```
HALF THE WORLD AWAY
(Gallagher)
from the single "Whatever"
{Intro}:   C   F   (x3)
{Verse}:
C                   F
I would like to leave this city
C                    F
This old town don't smell too pretty and
C    Em      Am  (Aadd9)    D      Dsus4      D      F
I can feel the warning signs running around my mind
C         F                      C              F
And when I leave this island I'll book myself into a soul asylum
C      Em      Am  (Aadd9)    D      Dsus4      D      F
And I can feel the warning signs running around my mind
{Chorus}:
Am        C         E7                     Am   (Aadd9)
So here I go still scratching around the same old hole
F                        Fm         G    G7
My body feels young but my mind is very old
Am   (Aadd9)         C
So what do you say?
        E7                          Am    (Aadd9)
You can't give me the dreams that are mine anyway
       F
You're half the world away
Fm
Half the world away
C        Em    Am
Half the world away
         D          Dsus4        D        F
I've been lost I've been found but I don't feel down.
{Verse 2}:
{same as Chorus chords}:
So here I go still scratching around in the same old hole
My body feels young but my mind if very old
So what do you say?
You can't give me the dreams that are mine anyway
You're half the world away
Half the world away                          Fadd9
Half the world away
I've been lost I've been found but I don't feel down
{Outro}: C  F( or Fadd9)
```

The Great Songs of Cat Stevens.

Wise Publications
London/New York/Sydney

Exclusive Distributors:
Music Sales Limited,
8/9 Frith Street, London W1V 5TZ, England.
Music Sales Pty. Limited,
120 Rothschild Avenue, Rosebery, NSW 2018, Australia.

This book © Copyright 1984 by
Wise Publications
UK ISBN 0.7119.0564.9
UK Order No. AM37664

Compiled by Peter Evans.
Designed by Pearce Marchbank and Philip Levene.
Cover photography by L.F.I.

Music Sales complete catalogue lists thousands of titles
and is free from your local music book shop, or direct from
Music Sales Limited, 8/9 Frith Street, London W1V 5TZ.
Please enclose a cheque or postal order for £1.50 for postage.

Printed in England by
Halstan & Co. Ltd., Amersham, Bucks.

The Great Songs of Cat Stevens.

Father And Son.

Words & Music: Cat Stevens

Slowly

It's not time to make a change just re-lax take it eas-y, you're still
time to make a change just sit down take it slow-ly, you're still

young that's your fault there's so much you have to know Find a
young that's your fault there's so much you have to go through. Find a

girl set-tle down ___ if you want you can mar-ry, look at
girl set-tle down ___ if you want you can mar-ry, look at

4

still be here tomorrow but your dreams may not. How can

I try to ex-plain? When I do he turns a-way__ a-gain, It's

al-ways been the same, same old sto-ry. From the mo-ment I could talk I was

or-dered to lis - ten now there's a way_____ and I know that I

The First Cut Is The Deepest.

Words & Music: Cat Stevens

Wild World.

Words & Music: Cat Stevens

10

child, girl.____

Ba-by I love___ you, But if you want to leave___ take good

care, hope you make a lot of nice friends out there. But just re-mem-ber there's a lot of bad

D.S. 𝄉 al ⊕

and be - ware____

CODA ⊕

child, girl.____

12

Where Do The Children Play?

Words & Music: Cat Stevens

Moderately

13

14

play?____

Well you've cracked the sky scrap-ers fill the air but will you

keep on build - ing high-er till there's no more room up there will you

make us laugh, will____ you make us cry, will you

tell us when ___ to live ___ will you tell us   when to die?

I know we've come a long way   we're chang-ing day ___ to day. ___

But tell me where do the child-ren play? ___

Keep repeating and fade

Doo doo   doo   doo doo   doo doo   doo   doo doo.

Hard Headed Woman.

Words & Music: Cat Stevens

I'm looking for a hard headed woman, One who'll take me for __ my-

self.__ And if I find my hard head-ed wom - an __

I won't need _____ no - bod - y else, no, no, no. _____

I'm look- ing for a hard head-ed wom- an,

one who will make me feel so good, And if I find my hard head-ed

wom- an I know my life will be as it should, yes yes, yes

D.S. al Coda

Coda

Tuesday's Dead.

Words & Music: Cat Stevens

Fairly Bright Jamaican (in 2)

We must try___ to shake it down, Do our best__ to break the ground,

try to turn___ the world a - round one more

time.___

2nd time
D.S. al Coda

⊕ *CODA*

Tues - day's dead.___

Oh preacher won't you paint my dream
won't you show me where you've been,
show me what I haven't seen
to ease my mind
'Cause I will learn to understand
If I have a helping hand
I wouldn't make another demand, all my life
Whoa - where do you go when you don't
want no-one to know
Who told tomorrow - Tuesday's dead

What's my sex, what's my name,
all in all it's all the same
everybody plays a different game - that is all
Now man may live, man may die
searching for the question why,
but if he tries to rule the sky - he must fall
Whoa - where do you go when you don't
want no-one to know
Who told tomorrow - Tuesday's dead
Now every second on the nose
The humdrum of the city grows

25

Sad Lisa.

Words & Music: Cat Stevens

1. She hangs her head and cries on my shirt,
2. eyes like win-dows trick-el-ing rain,
3. (Instrumental)
4. sits in a cor-ner by the door,

she must be hurt ver-y bad-
up-on her pain get-ting deep-
there must be more I can tell

—ly,
—er,
—her,

Tell me what's mak-ing you
Though my love wants to re-
If she real-ly wants me to

Maybe You're Right.

Words & Music: Cat Stevens

I put up ___ with your lies like ___ you put up with mine, ___ But God knows we

should have stopped some-where, ___ we could have tak-en the time, ___ But time has

hap-pen a-gain,___ Nev-er, nev-er,_nev-er, It -'ll nev-er hap-pen a-gain_

No, no, no, no, no, _____ no, no, no, no, no.

D.S. al ⊕ Coda

CODA

pp

33

Morning Has Broken.

Words: Eleanor Farjeon
Music: Cat Stevens

1.4. Morn - ing has brok - en like the first morn -
2. Sweet the rain's new fall, sun - lit from heav -

3. Mine is the sun - light, Mine is the morn -

ing, Born of the one light E - den saw play.

Praise with e - la - tion, Praise ev - 'ry morn -

ing, God's re - cre - a - tion of the new day.

I Wish, I Wish.

Words & Music: Cat Stevens

Moderately

1. I wish I knew, I wish I knew _____
2. I wish I could tell, I wish I could tell _____

what makes me, me, what makes you, you. _____ It's just an-
what makes a heaven what makes a hell. _____ And do I

oth- er point of view _____ oo _____ A state of
get to ring my bell _____ oo _____ Or land up

Lady d'Arbanville.

Words & Music: Cat Stevens

and you will be my fill, Yes, you will be my fill. My

La-dy d'Ar-ban-ville   why does it grieve me so?

But your heart seems so si-lent,   Why

do you breathe so low why do you breathe so low, my La-dy d'Ar-ban-ville
2. I loved you my la-dy

7/98 (31456)

The Great Songs of George Harrison.

ISBN 0.7119.0562.2
Order No. AM37649

The Great Songs of Chris De Burgh.

ISBN 0.7119.0464.2
Order No. AM35536

The Great Songs of Michael Jackson.

ISBN 0.7119.0483.9
Order No. AM36401

The Great Songs of Stevie Wonder.

ISBN 0.7119.0421.9
Order No. AM34596

The Great Songs of The Police.

ISBN 0.7119.0550.9
Order No. AM37565

The Great Songs of Al Stewart.

ISBN 0.7119.0666.1
Order No. AM39587

The Great Songs of John Denver.

ISBN 0.7119.0563.0
Order No. AM37656

The Great Songs of The Carpenters.

ISBN 0.7119.0638.6
Order No. AM39108

The Great Songs of Barry Manilow.

ISBN 0.7119.0561.4
Order No. AM37631

The Great Songs of Cat Stevens.

ISBN 0.7119.0564.9
Order No. AM37664

The Great Songs of The Rolling Stones.

The Great Songs of Rod Stewart.

ISBN 0.7119.0593.2
Order No. AM38225

ISBN 0.7119.0680.7
Order No. AM39694

The Great Songs of Chicago.

ISBN 0.7119.0681.5
Order No. AM39702

The Great Songs of Gordon Lightfoot.

ISBN 0.7119.0391.3
Order No. AM34109

The Great Songs of Chris De Burgh.

ISBN 0.7119.0697.1
Order No. AM 39900

Great Songs, Great Series.

*The greatest songs by the greatest
performers and songwriters of our times.
A handsomely presented, very collectable set of beautifully engraved music,
all in full piano/vocal arrangements with complete lyrics,
guitar chord boxes and symbols.
The most economical way of buying sheet music today.*

*Available from your local music dealer,
or contact...
Music Sales Limited,
8/9 Frith Street,
London W1V 5TZ.*